128 Tips *for* K-12 Teachers

Marcia Millet, Ed.D.

www.TrueVinePublishing.org

128 Tips for K-12 Teachers
Marcia Millet, Ed.D.

Published by
True Vine Publishing Company
810 Dominican Dr.
Nashville TN 37228
www.TrueVinePublishing.org

ISBN: 978-1-968092-57-3 Paperback
ISBN: 978-1-968092-58-0 eBook

Printed in the United States of America.
For information, contact the author at:
milletandassociates.com

Dedication

This book is dedicated to all the students, parents, grandparents, principals, custodians, secretaries, pre-service teachers, in-service teachers, and mentors who have shaped my journey. To the professors at Bennett College for Women who laid my educational foundation, at The Ohio State University who prepared me to teach in a global society, at Tennessee State University who believed in my ability to teach and transform beginning teachers' perceptions of teacher education, at Stillman College who afforded me the opportunity to serve as Associate Dean and Director of Teacher Education, and at Harvard University who provided me with leadership training through the Women in Education Leadership program, I give my profound thanks. My educational experiences have given me limitless opportunities to become the educator and administrator I am today.

I want to say a special thank you to my husband, Dr. Peter Edmund Millet, and my daughter, Dr. Mackenzie Janelle Millet, for believing in me and encouraging me to reach for the stars. To my beloved mother, Mrs. Minnie Rosalee Moose Strong, thank you for laying the foundation for my success.

Table of Contents

Teacher Resources

- Teacher-Friendly Education Glossary
- Artificial Intelligence Toolkit for Teachers
- Recommended Books by Category
- Subject-Specific Resources
- Websites
- Teacher Discounts

Dear New Teacher,

This book was written for you because you are about to embark on one of the most impactful and rewarding careers in the world. Your love for the profession and serving others will have a profound impact on you and your communities. Without you, there will be no doctors, lawyers, teachers, astronauts, physicists, or Nobel laureates. In this book, I'm sharing tips from thirty-five years of K-12 and higher-education teaching experience. These are tips that I wish someone had told me when I began my educational journey. It's my hope that they will empower you and enhance your teaching career. Get ready to change the world.

Sincerely,

Marcia Millet, Ed. D.

"Success is not defined by grades alone."
- Dr. Marcia Millet

What This Book Is About

This isn't your typical education textbook filled with complicated theories and lengthy explanations. Instead, it's a collection of practical tips gathered from over three decades of classroom experience working with students, parents, administrators, and fellow teachers. Each tip comes from real situations I've encountered, and strategies I've refined through years of trial, error, and success.

The book is organized into fifteen sections that cover essential aspects of your teaching career: Teachers, Student Involvement, School Environment, Parents, Differentiated Instruction, Classroom Management, Assessment, Technology, Professional Development, Mindset, Partnerships and Collaboration, Community, Research, Health and Wellness, and Money Management. This comprehensive approach ensures you'll find practical guidance for almost any situation you may encounter in your teaching journey.

Many years ago, I stood exactly where you're standing now, feeling excited, overwhelmed, and eager to make a difference. I understand what new teachers truly need: quick, practical advice that works in real classrooms with real kids.

Think of this book as your teaching toolkit. Please flip to the appropriate page when you need quick advice and keep it handy for those "what do I do now?" moments. I encourage you to share the tips with other new teachers. These aren't just theories, they're battle-tested strategies from thirty-five years of classroom experience that will make your teaching life easier and more effective. They're tips I wish I had known when I started my teaching journey.

The book also includes dedicated journal pages where you can record your own insights, reflect on which tips work best in your unique classroom setting, and document your growth as an educator. Your teaching journey is personal, and having space to capture your thoughts and experiences makes this book truly yours.

The Heart of This Book: You're Not Alone

Every tip in this book comes with an underlying message from someone who has truly been there. You're going to be great at this, and it's okay that you don't have everything figured out yet. After thirty-five years in education, I vividly remember my first years, the sleepless nights, the small victories, the moments of doubt, and the incredible joy of watching students learn and grow.

These tips aren't from textbook theories, they're from real moments in real classrooms, from mistakes I made and lessons I learned, from strategies that evolved over decades of working with thousands of students.

Sample Tips from the Book

Tip #3: Balance Your Professional and Personal Lives
Balance your professional life with your personal life. Minimize taking papers home to grade every night/weekend. You need to have a full and robust life outside of the classroom. Go to a movie, visit a shopping center, exercise, participate in religious services, spend time with family and friends, and by all means, keep your scheduled medical appointments. Develop a schedule that's authentic.

Tip #20: Display Work from All of Your Students

Display work from students at all stages of the performance spectrum. Avoid displaying only work that's considered "good." All students have talents. Keep a log of students' work. Students are very aware of whose work gets displayed and whose does not. Seeing their work displayed publicly will instill in them a sense of pride.

Tip #27: Attend After-School Events

If a student invites you to an event, always try to attend, even if you can't stay for the entire program. They'll remember your support for them many years down the road. In some cases, you may be the only person to show up and support them.

Tip #44: Flip the Parent-Teacher Conference

During parent-teacher conferences, the student should lead the discussion. This will allow them to take ownership of their academic success and show their parents how much they know. The norm is for the teacher to lead, but this flipped conference model is a useful alternative.

Tip #107: Present at Local, Regional, and National Conferences

Collaborate with a local college or university on research projects. It's important for college professors to understand educational issues from the perspective of practicing educators. Presenting at conferences gives you the opportunity to share your expertise and strengthen the connection between theory and practice. Your real-world experience makes you an invaluable resource.

Why These Tips Work

1. They're Specific: Rather than giving you vague advice like, "build relationships," you get concrete actions such as, "learn something personal about each student and reference it in conversation."

2. They're Realistic: These tips acknowledge that you're busy, tired, and learning on the job. They're designed to help. These tips won't add any unnecessary work to your plate.

3. They're Tested: Every tip comes from my thirty-five years of classroom experience. They're strategies I've personally tried, refined, and seen work across different grade levels, subjects, and student populations.

4. They're Real: These tips emerged from actual classroom situations, not educational theory. They've been tested by time, by diverse student needs, and by changing educational landscapes.

These practical tips can be adapted for any grade level or subject area.
Remember, good teaching principles translate.

Tips on How to Use This Book

This is a user-friendly book with simple, memorable advice you can use immediately. Written by a teacher for teachers. It includes journal pages for reflection and personal insights.

- Morning Coffee Reading: Read 2-3 tips with your morning coffee for quick inspiration and ideas.

- Problem-Solving Tool: When facing a specific challenge, flip through for relevant tips.

- Collaboration Starter: Share tips with colleagues to build and strengthen your teaching community.

- Weekend Reflection: Read a few tips on Saturday or Sunday while planning your week, then jot down your thoughts in the journal section.

- Personal Growth: Use the journal pages to document which tips you've tried and how they've worked in your specific classroom.

- Emergency: Keep this book handy for those moments when you need immediate help.

Your Teaching Journey Begins

This book is full of practical advice ranging from how to organize your desk to how to manage difficult conversations. After thirty-five years of teaching, I want to share that for every challenge you're facing, I've faced them, too, and survived (and thrived). Your unique personality and approach are your greatest assets. The purpose of this book is to encourage and support your teaching journey. I want you to succeed because I remember what it was like to be new.

This book is a compilation of the advice I wish I'd received when I first started teaching. It won't solve every challenge you'll face, but it'll make your daily life easier and remind you that you're part of an incredible profession.

Some days you'll flip through looking for specific help. Other days you'll read a tip and think, "I already do that!" (which means you're developing good instincts). At other times you'll find exactly the encouragement you need to remember why you became a teacher in the first place.

Most importantly, this book reminds you that becoming a great teacher is a journey, not a destination. It's a long-distance run, not a sprint. Every tip you try, every small improvement you make, and every student you connect with, is part of that journey. After three decades of this work, I can tell you with certainty that you're exactly where you need to be, and you're going to be amazing.

The best teachers aren't the ones who never struggle, they're the ones who keep learning, keep caring, and keep showing up for their students. That's doing exactly what you're doing, and it's exactly why you're going to be great. Great teaching isn't about perfection, it's about connection, growth, and the willingness to try one more time. These suggestions will help guide you on your journey toward becoming the teacher you've always aspired to be.

Section 1

Teachers: The Heart of the Classroom

TIP #1

Teach with Love:

Teach as if every student is "your" child, brother, sister, niece, cousin, godchild, etc. How would you want your family members to be treated by their teachers, even during challenging circumstances? That should inform your treatment of other peoples' children.

TIP #2

Be Flexible:

It's okay if you don't manage to cover everything you had planned to teach on a particular day. Base your teaching on mastery and not on the clock.

TIP #3:

Balance Your Professional and Personal Lives:

Balance your professional life with your personal life. Minimize taking papers home to grade every night/weekend. You need to have a full and robust life outside of the classroom. Go to a movie, visit a shopping center, exercise, participate in religious services, spend time with family and friends, and by all means, keep your scheduled medical appointments. Develop a schedule that's authentic.

TIP #4

Be Professional:

Always allow your students to observe you in a positive manner (the way you dress, treat others, speak, etc.). They're watching and mirroring you, even when you don't know they are.

TIP #5

Accountability:

Remember to never leave your students unattended. If you need to go to the restroom, office, library, etc., make sure another teacher is watching your students. It only takes a few seconds for something unexpected, and unwanted, to happen.

TIP #6

Planning Time:

Use your planning time to actually plan, either independently or collaboratively. Don't turn your planning period into a time for running errands and handling your personal affairs. Once started, this is an extremely hard habit to break and will end up shortchanging your students. (Also, often during this time, your principal will need to schedule student-related meetings.)

TIP #7

Teachers Night Out:

Establish a fun routine with your colleagues. Go out to eat, watch a movie, go thrift shopping, attend a football or basketball game, attend an art/craft show, go to a play or music concert, etc. Teachers need to have fun, too! If you establish a good rapport with your colleagues during the good times, they'll be there for you during the hard times.

TIP #8

Keep a Journal:

Keep a journal to document your daily triumphs and also your tribulations. On your most difficult days, you'll be able to go back and see all the obstacles you've overcome. Sometimes, when you're in the midst of a storm, it's hard to remember all that you've accomplished. On your good days, celebrate your accomplishments.

TIP #9

Be on Time:

Buy a reliable clock. Whether you use a traditional alarm clock or a cellular device, being on time is a good habit. Develop a reputation for always being on time and show up five minutes early for your appointments. Think of it this way: To be early is to be on time; to be on time is to be late.

TIP #10

GPS:

Identify different routes to your job. Download traffic apps that'll identify high traffic volume. Without fail, on the days that you have someplace important to be, there will be a traffic delay causing you to be late.

TIP #11

Keep Your Car in Good Shape:

Get your car serviced according to the manufacturer's schedule, even when nothing is going wrong. Treat your car with respect! Don't wait for it to break down, be proactive.

TIP #12

Cherish the Memories:

Invest in a camera to document your success. If you take pictures with your phone, learn how to save them in the cloud. (Make sure that your students have a signed consent form prior to taking their pictures.)

TIP #13

Reflect Regularly:

It's important to reflect on your students, school, fellow teachers, parents, and yourself daily. It's easy to become so absorbed in your daily routine that you forget to pause and reflect on your actual actions. Reflection ensures that all matters are viewed with an objective and realistic perspective.

TIP #14

Building School Friendships:

Keep your personal life private. Gossip travels fast. Everyone who is a teacher is not your friend. Everyone who is in your circle is not in your corner. Avoid participating in gossip when you're in the teachers' lounge. Today it's about another teacher; tomorrow, it could be about you.

TIP #15

Protect Your Spiritual Health:

Making spiritual guidance a regular part of your routine can help support your overall well-being. Acknowledge that there's a power greater than yourself and seek direction, wisdom and kindness.

TIP #16

First Impressions:

Remember that you only get one chance to make a first impression. Make the most of it. Look good, smell good, be organized, be early, give direct eye contact, and offer a firm handshake.

TIP# 17

Dress to Impress:

Classic styles are a great investment. Stay away from fads and dress your age, not the age of your students. Exude professionalism and class. A classic wardrobe will last for many years.

TIP# 18

Ladies Attire:

Invest in a pair of pearl earrings and necklace. Pearls can dress up a basic outfit and are always appropriate. On the other hand, fight the urge to wear high heels and invest in a good pair of comfortable shoes. (You'll thank me for this at the end of a long week.)

TIP# 19

Gentlemen's Attire:

Invest in a white shirt, and a dark suit and tie. Also, keep a spare blazer and tie in your classroom. You never know when these items will come in handy.

Reflections

"Education is the key that unlocks the golden door to freedom."
- George Washington Carver

Section 2

Student Involvement: Every Student Matters

TIP #20

Display Work from All of Your Students:

Display work from students at all stages of the performance spectrum. Avoid displaying only work that's considered "good." All students have talents. Keep a log of students' work. They're very aware of whose work gets displayed and whose does not. Seeing their work displayed publicly will instill in them a sense of pride.

TIP #21

Literature and Writing:

No matter what content area you're teaching, include literature and writing. These content areas transcend all boundaries.

TIP #22

Eat With Your Class:

Instead of eating in the teachers' lounge every day, take time to eat and socialize with your students. They'll love this. Turn your classroom into a restaurant. Play music and teach dining etiquette. This approach also offers an excellent opportunity to understand each student on a more individual level.

TIP #23

Game Day:

Have a "Game Day." Students can play educational games to learn content. Allow students to create their own games. Use textbooks as springboards for creative activities, not as the only way to learn.

TIP #24

Tutoring:

Provide after-school tutoring for all students, not just those who are struggling. All students can grow academically. Also, have students tutor and help each other. They're smarter than you think. Those who aren't at the top of your grading chart often simply need an opportunity to demonstrate their potential.

TIP #25

Have High Expectations for Your Students:

All students should be encouraged to reach their highest potential. Raise the bar and they'll rise to meet your highest expectations. It doesn't matter where they come from, what matters is where they're going. Don't "dummy down" their work.

TIP #26

Sharing:

Don't be afraid to share your hobbies with your students and your school family. Celebrate your talents! Let them get to know a little about your life outside of the classroom.

TIP #27

Attend After-School Events:

If a student invites you to an event, always try to attend, even if you can't stay for the entire program. They'll remember your support for them many years down the road. In some cases, you may be the only person to show up and support them.

TIP #28

Get to Know Your Students:

Make it a priority to engage in daily conversations with each of your students. Regular, informal interactions allow you to identify emerging social or personal concerns early on, in a non-threatening manner. Establishing this rapport in advance creates a foundation of trust, which can be invaluable should a crisis or challenging situation arise.

TIP #29

Saturday School:

Invite parents and students to attend school one Saturday each month to engage in learning various academic subjects together. Base the lesson on the specific needs of the students. Make sure the environment is fun and non-threatening.

TIP #30

Class Newsletter:

Develop a newsletter that showcases your students' academic success. The newsletter could be provided either in an electronic format or as a printed version. It might even serve as a class project. Make sure to include students who are frequently overlooked and not usually considered leaders in the class.

TIP #31

Taking Responsibility for All Your Students' Academic Performance:

Don't blame last year's teachers, parents, or previous schools for achievement gaps. Your job is to accept students where they are and lead them to fulfill their potential. That's why you're sitting at the big desk.

TIP #32

Watch Out for Bullies:

Make sure that every student feels safe and secure in the classroom. Bullies can take away from this safe environment for some students. Watch out for students who have a change in behavior, demeanor, or mood. Be vigilant and always watch for students who are being mistreated. This mistreatment may take place in the classroom, the playground, or virtually. These students may not know what to say, what to do, or where to turn. They're depending on you to be their advocate.

Reflections

"There is a brilliant child locked inside every student."

- Marva Collins

Section 3

School Environment: School Culture and You

TIP #33

Attend School Board Meetings:

Stay abreast of what's happening in your school district. Stay actively involved in local, state, and national conversations. With your direct student experience, you're well-positioned to offer practical insights into classroom realities to individuals who may influence decision-making processes.

TIP #34

Show Your School Spirit:

Make T-shirts that display the school's name and motto. This can be a class or school project. Collaborate with a local printer to get the shirts donated. Have a student or a group of students design the T-shirt. Wear the shirts at special events. A little-known fact is that many local stores and vendors will donate goods and services for free, you just have to ask.

TIP #35

Plan a Scavenger Hunt:

It's important for students to become familiar with their school environment and history. Create a monthly scavenger hunt for them. Award school paraphernalia for the prizes.

TIP #36

Volunteer:

Get involved. Volunteer to make your school better! For example, arrive early and help the secretary. Give the secretary a break when he or she doesn't expect it. Assist with car or bus duty when it isn't your scheduled week. You don't need to be paid monetarily for everything you do. Compensation comes in many forms.

TIP #37

Schedule an Open House:

Have students design a personal postcard to send to their parents, grandparents, city council representatives, neighbors, etc., to invite them to the school's open house program. Many community members don't attend school activities simply because they haven't received an invitation.

TIP #38

Recognize the Staff:

The janitor, secretary, and cafeteria employees are important, too. Invite them to your class and publicly express your appreciation for all they do. Praise them in front of your students. They are also typically aware of everything happening at school, not just within the classroom but outside as well. They're great sources of information.

TIP #39

Involve Your School Principal:

Invite your principal to visit your class to see your students give oral reports, participate in hands-on lessons, or just stop by to say hello. Students should learn to see the principal as an ally, not someone to be feared.

TIP #40

Remain Vigilant When spending Time in the Teacher's Lounge:

It's okay to go to the teachers lounge; however, keep the conversation positive. Avoid negativity and criticism of others. Keep the discussion on general topics, such as sports, food, traveling, a new book, or a new movie. If the conversation turns negative, that's your signal to leave.

Reflections

"The culture of a school determines the culture of the classroom."

\- Todd Whitaker

Section 4

Parents: Partners in Learning

TIP #41

Send Parent Alert Communications:

A Parent Alert is a note that can be sent to parents at any time to inform them of concerns regarding their child. This note may be sent home via email or U.S. mail. A phone call or text message should also be made to inform the parent that an "alert" has been sent.

TIP #42

Establish a Book Club:

Establish a book club for parents and students. Choose a day of the week that works for everyone. In addition to providing an opportunity for students to practice their reading skills, it also provides time for students and parents to engage in academic endeavors together.

TIP #43

Host a Family Night:

Host a school Family Night for math, science, and reading. The event might include games, food, media, and more. This activity will allow parents to become even more involved in their child's learning. Make it a fun and educational night.

TIP #44

Flip the Parent-Teacher Conference:

During parent-teacher conferences, the student should lead the discussion. This will allow them to take ownership of their academic success and show their parents how much they know. The norm is for the teacher to lead the meeting, but this flipped-conference model is a useful alternative.

TIP #45

Invite Parents to be Guest Speakers:

Invite parents to share their experiences and personal expertise with the class. Parents enjoy visiting their child's class or school, and it's also a source of pride for their child.

TIP #46

Contact Parents Early:

All parents should be contacted one month before school begins via phone, mail, or email. By taking this action early before any potential problems arise, the teacher can establish a relationship that'll help parents feel more open to discussing future concerns should they arise.

Reflections

"What the best and wisest parent wants for his child, that must we want for all the children of the community. Anything less is unlovely, and left unchecked, destroys our democracy."
- John Dewey

Section 5

Differentiated Instruction: Meeting Children Where They Are

TIP #47

504, IEP, Accommodation, Modification:

Know the difference between a 504, an IEP, a Modification, and an Accommodation. Know when and how to use each.

- A **504 Plan** is developed for students who have a disability of some type but don't require special education services.

- An **Individualized Education Program (IEP)** is a legal document mandated by the Individuals with Disabilities Education Act (IDEA) that outlines the specialized instruction and services a child with a disability needs to succeed in school.

- **Accommodations** help students access the same curriculum as their peers by altering how they learn (e.g., different tools or settings for the same material).

- **Modifications** change what a student is taught or expected to learn, potentially altering learning goals (e.g., different curriculum or expectations).

TIP #48

Listen to Your Students:

Students learn from you, and you learn from your students. Give them opportunities to speak, and take the time to listen. While you're the content matter expert, they're the ultimate authorities on their own lives. You may be surprised by what you learn.

TIP #49

Demonstrate Culturally Responsive Teaching:

Get to know your students' backgrounds, values and lived experiences. This will allow you to make wise and informed decisions. Don't assume that all students of a particular racial or ethnic group, or religion, are alike. There will often be more differences within cultural groups than between them. You can understand students best by knowing how they think, rather than by how they look.

TIP #50

Make Real Life Connections:

Students need to understand that what they're learning in school applies to their real-life experiences. Allow them to see the connection. Do not just read from the textbook, give real-life examples. Bring lessons to life by showing how what they see or hear in the news applies to them.

TIP #51

Stay Current with Relevant Research:

Attend local, state, and national conferences on teacher-related issues to stay up to date on the latest and best practices in your field. If you're short on funding, ask the conference staff if they're accepting volunteers. Often, volunteers contribute a few hours of their time and, in return, receive complimentary admission to the conference. You just have to ask.

TIP #52

Actively Engage Your Students:

Teach in an engaging and fun way that includes all students. Think outside the box. Active participation helps students learn better than passive listening. Make sure to include the quiet or withdrawn student who sits in the last row at the back of the classroom.

TIP #53

Be Knowledgeable about Special Education:

If you aren't certified in special education, it's important to work collaboratively with resource teachers and local support agencies to stay abreast of current policies and strategies to meet your students' diverse needs. Students in special education classes have great potential for success, just like all of your other students. They rely on you to support them and hold them to high standards.

TIP #54

**Support English Language Learners
and Their Parents:**

Modify your lessons so that English Language Learners (ELLs) are working to their greatest potential. Collaborate with local school systems, colleges, and universities to communicate with parents and secure translated materials for families. Whenever possible, arrange for an interpreter to be present at parent-teacher conferences. Ensure that letters and communications that are sent home have been appropriately translated. If you're so motivated, consider learning a second language yourself. This will strengthen your connection with the students and help them to feel included.

TIP #55

Pace Your Teaching:

It's important to teach according to your students' strengths and weaknesses, not strictly according to your lesson plan. It's more important that students learn than it is for you to finish a unit of work on time.

TIP #56

Teach in Different Ways That Support How Students Learn:

Students are different, and they learn differently. Take the time to get to know your students. In the long run, it'll save time, and your students will be more likely to succeed. Study and learn about the different types of learners, including visual, auditory, kinesthetic, logical/analytical, social/linguistic, and naturalistic.

Reflections

"The single greatest effect on student achievement is not race, it is not poverty, it is the effectiveness of the teacher".

- Harry Wong

Section 6

Classroom Management: Creating Your Learning Sanctuary

TIP #57

Discipline with Compassion and Understanding:

If a student does something inappropriate, try to find out the *why* before casting judgment and applying sanctions. Remember, there are three sides to every story: version one, version two, and the truth.

TIP #58

Be Mindful when Placing Students:

During the first week of school, allow students to sit where they want. This will allow you to observe naturally occurring dynamics. Then, during the second week, create a seating chart based on your observations. Students need to learn how to work cooperatively. Remember, adjustments will need to be made throughout the year.

TIP #59

Recognize and Reward Your Students:

Allow your students to read to, and/or tutor a student in a lower grade. Depending on the grade and ability, give them the opportunity to help the principal or serve as the student leader for the day. Remember to identify a great quality in each of your students. Don't spend all your time with your top students. All students are important. Help them go from good, to better, to best.

TIP #60

Develop a Model for How Students Should Label Their Work:

Identify where you want students to place their name and date on written assignments. Model and display an example in the classroom which can serve as a model.

TIP #61

Arrange Your Room Thoughtfully:

Arrange desks and tables in a way that's safe, effective, and conducive to learning. Be flexible—if the seating arrangement doesn't work, don't force it. Get to know your students and ensure you aren't overlooking mandatory requirements.

TIP #62

Provide Quiet Time:

Every day, allow about ten minutes for your students to sit and reflect quietly on their day by writing in a journal. For some, this may be the only opportunity they have to gather their thoughts and make plans for the next day.

TIP #63

Play Music to Enhance the Atmosphere:

Playing music creates a relaxing and inviting atmosphere. Write the name of the artist on the board. Allow students to experience different genres of music. The music should be instrumental unless the lyrics are non-controversial (for example, *Twinkle, Twinkle Little Star,* multiplication raps, instrumental jazz, classical, or contemporary pieces). If there are lyrics, always make sure to play the "clean" version of songs.

TIP #64

Model Appropriate Classroom Procedures:

Practice and model what you want your students to do in the classroom and around the school. People tend to be guided more by your actions than by your words. You must not only talk the talk—you must walk the walk.

TIP #65

Identify Class Helpers:

Allow all of your students to help in class. They can peer-teach, write assignments on the board, water plants, and more. Leadership is for all students. Find the strengths of each student and empower them. Often, students who are perceived as challenging will blossom if given a chance to lead or to hold a seat of responsibility. Engage with all of your students, not just your "top" students.

TIP #66

Post an Inspirational Quote on Your Door:

Place a positive and inspiring quote on the outside of your door. This will allow students to enter the class with high expectations for the day. It's a daily reminder that, "Today is going to be a great day."

TIP #67

Personal Quotes on Student's Desks:

Laminate and tape a positive or motivational quote on each student's desk. This lets them know that you see them and value them as individuals. For example:

"Hold fast to dreams
for if dreams die
life is like a broken-winged bird
that cannot fly."
Langston Hughes

TIP #68

Tidy Your Space on a Daily Basis:

Clean your classroom every afternoon before leaving for the day. Returning to a cluttered space the next day sets the tone for confusion and suboptimal performance. An orderly space sets the tone for a productive day and gives an inviting appearance to others. It conveys pride and professionalism to others. Take a few minutes and clean up at the end of the day.

TIP #69

Plan Ahead for Substitutes:

Stay organized. Create and maintain a substitute folder by the first week of school and update it regularly. Don't forget to include information about students with special needs, as well as the locations of emergency information for fire, tornado, and safety drills. If you stay ready, you never have to get ready.

TIP #70

Build Vocabulary Daily:

Teach your students a new word every day. Have your students practice using the word in sentences, discussions, and with family. Using new words boosts language skills and self-confidence.

TIP #71

Say Thank You:

Keep a box of thank-you notes in your desk drawer. A handwritten note is a simple but powerful way to show appreciation. Handwritten notes are rarely sent, but always appreciated.

TIP #72

Start the Day with a Smile:

Greet your students every morning with a "good morning," a smile, or a welcoming ritual. Take the time to build a strong foundation daily. You never know what their home life is like. You may be the most encouraging person they see all day.

TIP #73

Use Exit Tickets for Reflection:

End the day by allowing your students to write a quick note to you to let you know how their day went. They may reflect on their learning, experiences, or just how they're feeling. It can be as simple as, *"Today's science experiment was fun."* Always give students time to reflect on the school day.

TIP #74

Add Life to Your Classroom with Plants:

Place at least three live plants in your classroom. Plants are good for the environment and are aesthetically pleasing. Students can also take turns watering the plants. Incorporate this into a lesson in responsibility and science.

TIP #75

Address Concerns Calmly and Promptly:

Always address unpleasant situations in a calm manner, but do so immediately. Don't react emotionally, but rather take time to understand the problem fully before responding. Be slow to anger, but don't delay your response. Addressing problems early prevents bigger challenges later.

Reflections

Section 7

Assessment: Beyond the Gradebook

TIP #76

Assess Early and Often

Assessing your students regularly will give you the real "picture" of how they learn and where they are academically. Start on the first day of school, not just through formal tools, but also through informal observations and conversations with students. Get to know what type of learners your students are and plan accordingly.

TIP #77

Maintain Electronic Grade Records:

Use an electronic grading system to record your grades and monitor student progress. In addition to being efficient, depending on the system, you may be able to detect patterns and trends that will inform your instruction. Using paper recording techniques may prove problematic as those types of records are subject to being lost and are difficult to maintain over the long term.

TIP #78

Let Data Inform Instruction:

Use authentic data to drive instruction as opposed to relying solely on anecdotal notes or casual observations. Data-informed instruction helps you identify gaps and trends, and modify your instruction based on your analysis of the data.

TIP #79

Create a System for Data Collection:

Develop a data-collection system that works for you, either manual or digital. If you use a manual process, start with a three-ring binder. Using dividers, label each tab with a student's name. Place ruled paper behind each tab. Keep the notebook on your desk and use it to quickly and regularly record information in real time. The information collected should be used to make informed decisions. If you have the skill set and resources, this may also be done electronically. The important thing is to have a consistent system for collecting data and using it to improve student outcomes. Regularly enter data into the system in real time. If you wait until the end of the week to enter data, you may forget critical information or become preoccupied with other tasks and fail to enter the data at all.

Reflections

"Not everything that can be counted counts, and not everything that counts can be counted."

- Albert Einstein

Section 8

Technology: Embracing the Digital Classroom

TIP #80

Stay Current with Technology:

Keep up with the latest technology. Ask your principal to invite a technology expert to your school to share best practices and demonstrate how to effectively use technological equipment to bolster your in-class instruction. Take professional development courses to stay updated on the newest platforms and technology tools used in your industry. You don't want to be left behind.

TIP #81

Use Social Media Responsibly:

Use social media cautiously. Be careful about who you invite to be a friend and be careful about what you post on social media platforms. Nothing is 100 percent safe or private. Assume that whatever you put on social media will be viewed by students, colleagues, administrators, parents, and even future employers. Once you post something, assume it may be present online forever.

TIP #82

Create a Classroom Webpage:

Communicate with your students, parents, and guardians by creating a personal webpage using Google or another free platform. This webpage may be used to share information with your students and their parents as well as provide useful resources for families.

TIP # 83

Make Cybersecurity and Student Privacy a Priority:

Familiarize yourself with school policies and procedures regarding student privacy and online data security. Be aware of Family Educational Rights and Privacy Act (FERPA) guidelines and teach students about online safety.

TIP #84

Make Backups of Your Work Regularly:

Use cloud storage to save lesson plans, student grades, classroom planning documents, and other important work. Failure to back up your work could result in you losing your work due to any number of unexpected occurrences.

Reflections

"Technology will not replace great teachers, but technology in the hands of great teachers can be transformational."

- George Couros

Section 9

Professional Development: Never Stop Learning

TIP #85

Find a Mentor:

Find a positive and knowledgeable mentor. Ask someone to record you while you teach, then review the video together to discuss what you do well and where you can improve. Practice self-reflection daily.

TIP #86

Become a Lifelong Learner:

Consider going back to school and pursuing an advanced degree or specialized certificate. Since knowledge is always increasing, it's important to keep learning and growing as an educator. In education, to remain static is to be left behind.

TIP #87

Attend a Grant-Writing Workshop:

There are many funding opportunities available to help teachers build their classrooms, secure resources, and offer programs at their schools. Many school systems offer free grant writing workshops for teachers. Collaborating with other teachers is a necessary first step. Work with an experienced grant writer at your school, or in your district, and learn how to successfully apply for external funds. Granting agencies rarely support the lone-wolf grant writer; collaboration is the name of the game.

TIP #88

Read, Read, Read:

Keep up with the latest trends and research in education. Maintain a classroom library for your students to use during free reading time. Model this practice by reading yourself. Reading will help you remain aware of the best practices in your field.

TIP #89

Implement What You Learn:

Once you've gained new knowledge, either by personal reading, conference attendance, or other means, make sure that you actually put this new information into practice. Having knowledge and not using it for improvement isn't a good use of time. Find creative ways to put it into practice.

TIP #90

Learn a New Language:

Pursue opportunities to learn a second language. Many local community centers offer foreign language instruction at a discount, or even free of charge (particularly for teachers). Expanding your language skills will enrich your teaching and allow you to connect with diverse learners and their families.

Reflections

"Education is the most powerful weapon we have to
change the world."
- Nelson Mandela

Section 10

Mindset: Teacher First, Educator Always

TIP #91

Identify Teacher Pen Pals:

Establish connections with teachers in other schools, districts, cities, or states with whom you can communicate and collaborate. Teacher-to-teacher interaction is a great way to network and gather new and exciting ideas. This can be done through the internet, U.S. mail, or teacher blogs.

TIP #92

Utilize Professional Development Days:

Many school districts provide teachers with a set number of professional development days each year. It's important to use these days to seek out useful workshops that'll enhance your professional growth. Never say there are no good workshops available. You just have to look for them. They're out there.

TIP #93

Professional Organizations:

Join professional teacher organizations at the local, regional, and/or national levels. This will give you the opportunity to network, stay informed about the latest trends in education, and remain energized and empowered.

Reflections

"The size of your dreams must always exceed your current capacity
to achieve them. If your dreams do not scare you, they
aren't big enough."
- Ellen Sirleaf Johnson

Section 11

Partnerships and Collaboration: Building Your Support Network

TIP #94

Provide Transportation for After-School Meetings and Tutoring:

Work with principals, school districts, and community foundations to provide transportation for parents who need assistance if they are to attend after-school meetings. In some situations, the reason parents miss after school meetings or conferences is because they don't have a way to get to the school. Write a grant or collaborate with local churches, universities, and other organizations to secure vehicles. Make sure all bus drivers have passed background checks.

TIP #95

Offer Childcare Service:

Providing childcare on-site can bolster attendance and increase parent participation. Partnering with a local college or university can be beneficial in this area. Make sure all caregivers have passed background checks and hold certifications in CPR.

TIP #96

Establish Partnerships With Institutions of Higher Education:

Form partnerships with local colleges or universities to strengthen your school community. For example, if you need help with a newsletter, contact the English department. For science-related activities, connect with the science department. For Family Math Night, recruit students from math departments or math-methods courses to help plan and participate. Colleges and universities often have surplus supplies and equipment they're eager to donate. Often, you just need to ask.

TIP #97

Plan as Part of a Team:

Hold Professional Learning Community meetings with your teaching team. Throughout the school year, extend invitations to teachers from both the grade level above and the grade level below. This strategy allows teachers to prepare, plan, and reflect together on their current teaching practices. The curricula of teachers in the grades above and below your grade should be aligned.

TIP #98

Seek Out Nearby Teachers in Your Neighborhood:

Build connections with teachers who live nearby. For example, this can be helpful if you have car trouble and need a ride home or for carpooling. Likewise, you may be able to help them if the need ever arises.

TIP #99

Be a Team Player:

Work collaboratively with your team of teachers. Share your resources and support each other. Identify projects you can do collaboratively. Look for opportunities to support your colleagues without being asked.

TIP #100

Provide Treats in the Teacher Lounge:

Collaborate with another teacher to bring in treats for fellow staff members. Encourage others to do the same. This can create a pleasant escape at the end of a long day or a welcome break at any point during the day.

Reflections

"If you want to go fast, go alone. If you want to go
far, go together."

\- African Proverb

Section 12

Community: Building Your Village

TIP #101

Create a Community Garden:

Create a garden for your class or school and use it as a teachable project. For example:

- **Mathematics:** Measure how far apart to plant seeds.

- **Science:** Study soil types and plant growth.

- **Literacy:** Read and write about different kinds of plants.

- **Technology:** Take a virtual field trip to a botanical garden.

- **Community Outreach:** Students and parents can help maintain and use the garden.

- **Partnerships:** Work with local nurseries and colleges or universities to support and maintain the garden.

TIP #102

Enjoy Game Day:

Get students involved in local sports within the community. Host a class or school tailgate party. Reframe the event as a math lesson where students make predictions about which team will win, keep statistics, and track results. You might also reach out to local college or professional athletes to see if they're willing to visit. Most teams have community engagement offices that are eager to partner with schools. Many will donate tickets, clothing, or other team items. Often, you just need to ask.

TIP #103

Engage Students in Community Service:

Learn what partnerships already exist in your community and involve your students in service opportunities. Establish a system that'll allow students to keep track of their hours. This can be very helpful when they're applying for graduation or scholarships as it provides documentation that strengthens letters of reference. It's also useful to help students understand the value of helping others and the importance of thinking of the greater good. Additionally, when students volunteer or help others, it'll give them a great feeling of pride and confidence.

TIP #104

Stay Connected with Your Local School Board:

Attend school board meetings to stay informed about what's happening in your local school district. See if it's possible for you to become a member of the board.

TIP #105

Share the Good News:

At faculty meetings, encourage your principal to highlight the positive things happening in your school and various teachers' classrooms. For example, the principal might comment on a teacher who achieved 100 percent participation at Open House, or a teacher who received an award from their church, sorority, fraternity, or another organization. Recognizing these successes builds morale and community.

TIP #106

Network with Others:

Seek opportunities to socialize and connect with individuals in your social clubs and professional organizations. Networking strengthens relationships and has the potential to provide valuable resources and support to your classroom or school.

Reflections

"Education is not preparation for life; education is life itself."
- John Dewey

Section 13

Research: Practical Research Tips for Teachers

TIP #107

Present at Local, Regional, and National Conferences:

Collaborate with a local college or university on research projects. It's important for college professors to understand educational issues from the perspective of practicing educators. Presenting at conferences gives you the opportunity to share your expertise and strengthen the connection between theory and practice. Your real-world experience makes you an invaluable resource.

TIP #108

Highlight Contributors to Education:

Highlight an important person who has made a difference in education. This activity helps students develop an appreciation for individuals who have shaped, or are shaping, the field of education. Incorporate this throughout the school year to inspire and inform.

TIP #109

Maintain Political Awareness:

Stay informed about what's occurring in your state department of education and in the United States Department of Education. Consider how these developments might impact your school or district. It's beneficial to have relationships and awareness in the political world. Listen to podcasts, join list-serves, go to community meetings. Find ways to stay connected and informed.

TIP #110

Understand NAEP Scores:

NAEP refers to the National Assessment of Educational Progress, often called *The Nation's Report Card.* It measures student achievement in core subjects like reading and math in the United States. NAEP provides nationally representative data to monitor education trends, compare performance across states, and inform policy decisions. Assessments are given to students in grades 4, 8, and 12 to show what students know and can do, but they aren't used to determine individual results.

Stay informed about your state's status with NAEP. The NAEP website contains a wealth of information disaggregated by grade, race, sex, state, and other factors. This data is a valuable resource for understanding student performance and educational trends. (https://nces.ed.gov/nationsreportcard/)

Reflections

"The best teachers are those who show you where to look, but don't tell you what to see."

- Alexandra K. Trenfor

Section 14

Health and Wellness: Self-Care

TIP #111

Humor: The Free (and Legal) Stress Reliever:

Embrace laughter and joy while teaching. It's okay to laugh, smile, and enjoy your work. If you make a mistake, it's even okay to laugh at yourself. Your students and colleagues will respect you even more for your genuineness and authenticity.

TIP #112

Make the Most of Lunch Breaks:

During your breaks, slowly eat your lunch and listen to music to relax. Don't gobble it down so you can get to the next meeting. Avoid skipping lunch to complete work-related tasks. Take lunch at your designated time. This will maximize your work-life balance.

TIP #113

Do Not Teach While Angry:

Don't go to school angry, because you may take it out on your students, colleagues, or parents. Leave your anger and problems in the parking lot, or better yet, at home. There should be an emotional separation between your work and personal lives.

TIP #114

Make Maintaining Your Health a Priority:

Visit your physician and dentist regularly. Maintain a regular exercise routine, consume a balanced diet, and limit your intake of processed and fast foods. If necessary, see a counselor or therapist to help you address any emotional or mental challenges you may be experiencing that might negatively affect your work.

TIP #115

Pamper Yourself:

Manicures, pedicures, facials, massages, vacations, movies, golfing, playing basketball, and other activities are not luxuries, but necessities. Incorporate them into your routine. Activities like these serve to reinvigorate your mind, body, and spirit.

TIP #116

Read Poetry for Inspiration:

Read poems that inspire and empower you to listen to your inner self. This will stimulate your creativity and support your emotional well-being.

TIP #117

Wear Comfortable Shoes:

Invest in a pair of comfortable shoes that can be worn throughout the school year. Comfortable and supportive footwear contributes to physical health and classroom stamina.

TIP #118

Display Family Values:

Keep family photos of your pets, children, friends, vacations, graduations, and other moments. These constant reminders of the important things in life serve as motivation and grounding throughout the school day.

TIP #119

Expand Students' Horizons through Travel:

Allow your students to see the world through your eyes. Visit a city, state, or country virtually. Invite guest speakers, or, if resources allow, take an actual trip with your students. For some students, this might be their only chance to see more of what the world has to offer.

TIP #120

Engage in Regular Exercise:

Join a gym or local community center that offers discounts for educators in your neighborhood. Consider fitness options such as line dancing, tai chi, yoga, or Pilates to maintain physical health and reduce stress.

TIP #121

Create an Inspiring and Motivating Classroom:

Fill your classroom with positive words and posters. Keep yourself and your students encouraged. Strive to create and maintain an uplifting atmosphere.

Reflections

"Watch your thoughts, they become your words; watch your
words, they become your actions; watch your actions, they
become your habits; watch your habits, they become your
character; watch your character, it becomes your destiny."

- Lao Tzu

Section 15

Money Management: Financial Literacy for Educators

TIP #122

Keep a Loose-Change Jar:

Keep a container at home that's designated for loose change. Use this money to periodically purchase special treats or supplies for your students or classroom. (You'll be surprised at how much money can fit into a mayonnaise jar.)

TIP #123

Ask for Teacher Discounts:

Search the web for teacher discounts and always ask for these discounts at stores, restaurants, movies, theme parks, car dealerships, and any place else that you spend money. Many establishments and major brands have discounts for teachers; you often only need to ask. Here are a few options (do your own due diligence and research when using web-based sites):

- Teacher Discounts (shop.id.me)

- Teacher Discounts (myeducationdiscount. com)

- Teacher Perks (teacherperks.com)

TIP #124

Bargain Shop:

Shop at thrift stores and yard sales to find classroom bargains. These budget-friendly venues often provide great products for your classroom (or your closet) at very reasonable prices.

TIP #125

Save Your Money:

Start contributing to a retirement plan as soon as you receive your first paycheck, regardless of the amount. Try to increase your contribution each year. Retirement will be here before you know it, and you'll be glad that you started saving early.

TIP #126

Pay It Forward:

Consider establishing a scholarship fund for a student who plans to pursue a degree in education. Doing so will contribute to the development of the next generation of educators.

TIP #127

Don't Withdraw Retirement Funds Early

If you must relocate to another state, don't withdraw your retirement funds early. Keeping your benefits accruing interest will provide substantial long-term benefits. You'll be grateful for this decision thirty years from now.

TIP #128

Learn About Stocks and Bonds:

Start a teacher investment club at your school to promote financial literacy and retirement planning. Ask a local bank or teacher credit union for the name of a stockbroker. Learn about stocks, bonds, and investing. Preparing for retirement should begin as early as possible.

Reflections

"Do not save what is left after spending, but spend what is left after saving."

- Warren Buffett

Paying It Forward

Please write at least one tip that has been helpful to you that was not mentioned in this book. Feel free to submit it through our website at milletandassociates.com. It may be included in future editions of this book.

Thank you for taking the time to read my book. Have a wonderful school year!

Marcia J. Millet, Ed.D.

Teacher Resources

Teacher-Friendly Education Glossary

Teaching today requires fluency in an ever-expanding vocabulary of educational terms, frameworks, and approaches. From understanding trauma-informed practices to navigating special education terminology, from implementing social-emotional learning to differentiating instruction, educators need clear, practical definitions that connect directly to classroom realities. This glossary serves as your comprehensive reference guide, translating complex educational concepts into teacher-friendly language that you can immediately apply to your practice.

Whether you're a new teacher building foundational knowledge, an experienced educator exploring trauma-informed approaches, or anyone seeking to better understand how students learn and heal, these definitions will help you speak confidently about educational practices while deepening your understanding of the students you serve. Each term is crafted with the classroom in mind, emphasizing practical application over academic theory, because great teaching happens when we truly understand both our content and our students.

A

Accommodations: Modifications to how students access, engage with, or demonstrate learning without changing the content or expectations. Examples include extended time, preferred seating, or alternative formats for materials.

Adverse Childhood Experiences (ACEs): Potentially traumatic events that occur in childhood, such as abuse, neglect, or household dysfunction. Understanding ACEs helps teachers recognize why some students may struggle with behavior, learning, or emotional regulation.

Affect Regulation: A student's ability to manage and control their emotional responses. Trauma-informed teachers help students develop these skills through consistent routines, calming strategies, and emotional vocabulary building.

Assessment: The process of gathering information about student learning through various methods (tests, projects, observations) to inform instruction and measure progress.

Authentic Assessment: Evaluation methods that mirror real-world applications of knowledge and skills, such as portfolios, presentations, or problem-solving tasks.

B

Behavior Intervention Plan (BIP): A formal plan that outlines specific strategies to address challenging behaviors, typically developed for students receiving special education services.

Bloom's Taxonomy: A framework for categorizing learning objectives from basic recall (remembering) to higher-order thinking (creating, evaluating, analyzing).

Brain-Based Learning: Teaching approaches that align with how the brain naturally learns, including the understanding that trauma can impact brain development and learning capacity.

C

Co-regulation: The process where teachers help students manage their emotions by staying calm themselves and providing supportive presence during difficult moments. Essential in trauma-informed practice.

Culturally Responsive Teaching: Instruction that recognizes, values, and builds upon students' cultural backgrounds and experiences to make learning more relevant and effective.

Cumulative Stress: The build-up of ongoing stressors that can overwhelm a student's ability to cope, particularly relevant for students who have experienced trauma.

D

Differentiation: Adjusting instruction to meet individual student needs through varied content, process, products, or learning environment.

Direct Instruction: A teacher-centered approach where information is presented explicitly and systematically, often through modeling and guided practice.

Dysregulation: When a student's emotional or behavioral responses are outside their normal range of control, often triggered by stress or trauma reminders.

E

Emotional Safety: Creating classroom environments where students feel secure expressing themselves without fear of judgment, ridicule, or emotional harm.

Equity: Providing each student with what they individually need to succeed, which may mean different resources or approaches for different students.

Executive Function: Mental skills including working memory, flexible thinking, and self-control that help students manage tasks and regulate behavior. Often impacted by trauma.

F

Fight, Flight, or Freeze Response: The body's automatic reaction to perceived threats. Trauma-informed teachers recognize these responses in student behavior and respond with understanding rather than punishment.

Formative Assessment: Ongoing evaluation during the learning process used to adjust instruction, such as exit tickets, quick checks, or observation notes.

G

Grace Period: Intentionally allowing students time to transition between activities or recover from overwhelming situations, particularly important for trauma-affected students.

Growth Mindset: The belief that abilities and intelligence can be developed through effort, good strategies, and learning from mistakes.

H

Hypervigilance: A state of heightened alertness to potential threats, common in students who have experienced trauma, which can interfere with learning and concentration.

I

Individualized Education Program (IEP): A legal document outlining special education services, accommodations, and goals for students with disabilities.

Inquiry-Based Learning: An approach where students ask questions, investigate, and construct their own understanding with teacher guidance.

L

Learning Disability: A neurological condition that affects how the brain processes information, impacting specific academic skills like reading, writing, or math.

Least Restrictive Environment (LRE): The principle that students with disabilities should be educated with non-disabled peers to the greatest extent possible.

M

Mindfulness: Practices that help students (and teachers) focus on the present moment and develop awareness of thoughts and feelings without judgment.

Multi-Tiered System of Supports (MTSS): A framework providing different levels of academic and behavioral support based on student needs, from universal supports to intensive interventions.

N

Neuroplasticity: The brain's ability to reorganize and form new neural connections throughout life, offering hope that trauma's impacts can be addressed through supportive relationships and experiences.

P

Positive Behavioral Interventions and Supports (PBIS): A framework for creating positive school environments through clear expectations, teaching appropriate behaviors, and acknowledging positive choices.

Psychological Safety: An environment where students feel safe to take risks, make mistakes, ask questions, and express concerns without fear of negative consequences.

R

Re-traumatization: The process of experiencing trauma responses again when exposed to reminders or similar situations. Trauma-informed teachers work to prevent this through thoughtful practices.

Restorative Justice: An approach to discipline that focuses on repairing harm and rebuilding relationships rather than punishment alone.

Resilience: The ability to bounce back from adversity, stress, or trauma. Can be developed through supportive relationships and skill-building.

S

Safe Space: A designated area or general classroom environment where students feel physically and emotionally secure, often including calming tools and clear boundaries.

Scaffolding: Temporary support provided to help students achieve tasks they cannot yet complete independently, gradually removed as competence increases.

Secondary Trauma: The emotional stress experienced by teachers and school staff from hearing about or witnessing students' traumatic experiences.

Self-Regulation: A student's ability to manage their emotions, behavior, and attention in response to different situations and demands.

Sensory Processing: How the nervous system receives and responds to sensory information. Some students, particularly those with trauma history, may have heightened or diminished sensory responses.

Social-Emotional Learning (SEL): The process of developing skills to understand and manage emotions, set goals, show empathy, and maintain positive relationships.

Summative Assessment: Evaluation at the end of an instructional unit to measure student achievement, such as final exams, projects, or standardized tests.

T

Trauma: The result of experiencing or witnessing events that are physically or emotionally harmful and have lasting effects on well-being and functioning.

Trauma-Informed Care: An approach that recognizes the widespread impact of trauma and integrates knowledge about trauma into policies, procedures, and practices to promote healing.

Trauma-Informed Practices: Specific teaching strategies that create safety, build trust, offer choices, encourage collaboration, and emphasize strengths rather than deficits.

Trauma Response: Physical, emotional, or behavioral reactions to trauma triggers, which may include withdrawal, aggression, difficulty concentrating, or emotional outbursts.

Trauma Triggers: Situations, sounds, smells, or experiences that remind someone of past trauma and may cause them to relive traumatic feelings or memories.

Trust-Building: Intentional actions to establish reliable, safe relationships with students, especially important for those who have experienced trauma or broken trust with adults.

U

Universal Design for Learning (UDL): A framework for designing instruction that's accessible to all learners from the start, providing multiple means of representation, engagement, and expression.

Upstander: Someone who speaks up or acts when they witness bullying or injustice, promoting a positive school climate.

V

Vicarious Trauma: See Secondary Trauma: The emotional impact on educators from exposure to students' traumatic experiences.

W

Window of Tolerance: The zone where a person can think clearly and respond appropriately to stress. Trauma can narrow this window, making it important for teachers to help students stay within or return to their optimal zone.

Wraparound Services: Comprehensive support services that address multiple needs of students and families, often coordinated between school and community resources.

Z

Zone of Proximal Development: The difference between what a student can do independently and what they can do with guidance and support from a teacher or peer.

Artificial Intelligence (AI) Toolkit

Teachers, think of AI as your teaching assistant. AI can assist with teacher tasks. However, it's important to review your school's AI policy and use school approved tools.

AI and Educational Technology Tools for Teachers

(Please note this is an abbreviated list. There are many AI-educational technology tools for teachers)

MagicSchool AI -

magicschool.ai 80+ teacher tools, lesson plans, assessments, IEPs, student tools

ChatGPT - chat.openai.com

Lesson planning, explanations, creative content, image generation

Claude - claude.ai

Complex explanations, reliable content, collaborative tone

Brisk Teaching - briskteaching.com

Works in Docs/Gmail, reading level changes, instant feedback

Eduaide.AI - eduaide.ai

110+ templates, research-based strategies, curriculum alignment

Canva - canva.com

Design templates, Magic Write AI, drag-and-drop interface

Quizlet - quizlet.com

Flashcards, study games, practice tests, AI-powered features

Kahoot - kahoot.com

Live game shows, self-paced challenges, real-time results

Jeopardy Labs - jeopardylabs.com

Create custom Jeopardy games, no login required, instant play

Grammarly - grammarly.com

AI writing assistant for students and teacher communications

Nearpod - nearpod.com

Interactive lessons with AI-powered assessments and analytics

TeacherMatic - teachermatic.com

AI generators for worksheets, rubrics, and lesson plans

Fetchy - fetchy.com

AI assistant with 50+ productivity tools for teachers

Khan Academy (Khanmigo) - khanacademy.org/khan-labs

AI math tutor provides personalized step-by-step help

Turnitin - turnitin.com

AI writing feedback and plagiarism detection

Eduaide.AI - eduaide.ai

Generate modified assignments and accommodations

Gizmos (ExploreLearning) - explorelearning.com

Interactive science and math simulations

Nearpod Science - nearpod.com

Interactive science lessons with AI assessments

Universe Sandbox - universesandbox.com

AI physics and space simulation

Diffit - diffit.me

Instantly creates differentiated materials at multiple levels

Books

Educational Equity and Social Justice

Jonathan Kozol

- "Death at an Early Age: The Destruction of the Hearts and Minds of Negro Children in the Boston Public Schools" - National Book Award winner describing systemic inequities.

- "Savage Inequalities: Children in America's Schools" - Powerful examination of funding and resource disparities.

- "Amazing Grace: The Lives of Children and the Conscience of a Nation" - Investigation of poverty and education in the South Bronx.

- "The Shame of the Nation: The Restoration of Apartheid Schooling in America" - Documentation of continuing segregation in schools.

- "Rachel and Her Children: Homeless Families in America" - Robert F. Kennedy Book Award winner on homelessness and education.

- "Fire in the Ashes: Twenty-Five Years Among the Poorest Children in America" - Long-term follow-up on students from disadvantaged communities.

- "An End to Inequality: Breaking Down the Walls of Apartheid Education in America"

Teacher Development and Educational Policy

Linda Darling-Hammond

- "The Right to Learn: A Blueprint for Creating Schools That Work" - Vision for learner-centered schools and systemic reform.

- "The Flat World and Education: How America's Commitment to Equity Will Determine Our Future" - Analysis of international education systems and equity challenges.

- "Preparing Teachers for a Changing World: What Teachers Should Learn and Be Able to Do" - Comprehensive guide to teacher preparation.

- "Getting Teacher Evaluation Right: What Really Matters for Effectiveness and Improvement" - Evidence-based approach to teacher assessment.

- "Beyond the Bubble Test: How Performance Assessments Support 21st Century Learning" - Alternative assessment strategies.

- "Empowered Educators: How High-Performing Systems Shape Teaching Quality Around the World" - International perspectives on teacher development.

- "Preparing Teachers for Deeper Learning" - Focus on developing critical thinking and problem-solving skills.

- "Teaching as the Learning Profession: Handbook of Policy and Practice" - Comprehensive resource on professional development.

Classroom Management and Culture

- "The First Days of School" by Harry Wong - Practical guide to establishing effective classroom procedures and routines that set the foundation for a successful school year.

- "Teach Like a Champion" by Doug Lemov - sixty-two concrete teaching techniques used by outstanding educators to create rigorous, positive classroom environments.

- "The Classroom Management Book" by Harry Wong - Strategies for preventing discipline problems and building productive classroom communities.

Pedagogy and Instruction

- "Understanding by Design" by Grant Wiggins and Jay McTighe - Backward design framework for curriculum planning, starting with learning outcomes and working backward to create meaningful instruction.

- "The Differentiated Classroom" by Carol Ann Tomlinson - Practical strategies for adapting instruction to meet diverse student needs through differentiated content, process, and products.

- "Visible Learning for Teachers" by John Hattie - Research-based teaching practices that have the greatest impact on student achievement, synthesized from over 800 studies.

Student Engagement and Motivation

- "Drive" by Daniel Pink - Explores intrinsic motivation through three key elements: autonomy, mastery, and purpose, showing why traditional rewards often fail.

- "Mindset" by Carol Dweck - Introduces growth mindset versus fixed mindset and how beliefs about intelligence impact student learning and achievement.

- "The Courage to Teach" by Parker Palmer - Reflective exploration of teaching as a personal journey, emphasizing authentic teaching and creating meaningful learning communities.

Assessment and Feedback

- "Formative and Shared Assessment" by Dylan Wiliam - Evidence-based strategies for using assessment to improve learning through frequent, low-stakes assessments and effective feedback.

- "Fair Isn't Always Equal" by Rick Wormeli - Challenges traditional grading practices and offers differentiated assessment approaches that better reflect actual student learning.

Educational Technology

- "The Tech-Savvy Teacher" by Betsy Potash - Practical guide for meaningfully integrating technology into classroom instruction with concrete examples and step-by-step instructions.

- "Ditch That Textbook" by Matt Miller - Encourages creative alternatives to traditional textbook instruction using digital tools and student-centered activities.

Subject-Specific Areas
Mathematics

- "Building Thinking Classrooms in Mathematics" by Peter Liljedahl - Research-based practices for creating math classrooms where students actively think and engage with mathematical concepts.

- "5 Practices for Orchestrating Productive Mathematics Discourse" by Margaret Smith and Mary Kay Stein - Framework for facilitating meaningful mathematical discussions that advance student learning.

- "Mathematical Mindsets" by Jo Boaler - Shows how all students can succeed in mathematics when taught with growth-mindset principles and positive approaches.

- "Number Talks" by Sherry Parrish - Daily math conversations that build number sense and computational fluency through shared mental math strategies.

Reading/Literacy

- "The Reading Strategies Book" by Jennifer Serravallo - Collection of over 300 research-based reading strategies organized by skill and reading level for differentiated instruction.

- "The Book Whisperer" by Donalyn Miller - Strategies for creating authentic reading communities and motivating students to develop lifelong love of reading.

- "Guided Reading" by Irene Fountas and Gay Su Pinnell - Framework for small-group reading instruction that meets students at their instructional level.

- "When Kids Can't Read, What Teachers Can Do" by Kylene Beers - Practical strategies for supporting struggling readers and building comprehension skills.

Science

- "The Sense of Wonder" by Rachel Carson - A beautiful, short book encouraging teachers to nurture children's innate curiosity about the natural world through observation and exploration.

- "Last Child in the Woods" by Richard Louv - Explores "nature-deficit disorder" and the critical importance of connecting children with the outdoors. Makes a compelling case for nature-based learning and addresses how lack of nature experience affects children's physical, emotional, and cognitive development. Essential reading for advocating outdoor education.

- "Teaching Science Through Trade Books" by Christine Anne Royce - Practical strategies for integrating quality children's literature into science lessons to make concepts more accessible and engaging.

- "Uncovering Student Ideas in Science" series by Page Keeley - Formative assessment probes that help teachers identify and address common misconceptions students have about scientific concepts.

Social Studies

- "Teaching What Really Happened" by James W. Loewen - Challenges teachers to move beyond textbook myths and teach more accurate, inclusive American history that engages critical thinking.

- "We Want to Do More Than Survive" by Bettina Love - Explores abolitionist teaching and how to make social studies education more culturally relevant and justice-oriented.

"The Big History of Civilizations" by Craig G. Benjamin - Provides sweeping context for world history that can help teachers see connections across time periods and cultures.

Physical Education

- "Spark: The Revolutionary New Science of Exercise and the Brain" by John Ratey - Explains the cognitive and emotional benefits of physical activity, helping PE teachers advocate for their subject's importance.

- "Teaching Games for Understanding" by Linda L. Griffin & Joy Butler - A tactical approach to teaching sports and games that emphasizes decision-making and problem-solving over just skill drills.

Art

- "Studio Thinking 2" by Lois Hetland et al. - Research-based framework identifying eight "studio habits of mind" that art education develops, from observation to persistence.

- "Beautiful Oops!" by Barney Saltzberg - A children's book that's perfect for teaching growth mindset in art mistakes can become creative opportunities.

English Language Arts (ELA)

- "The Book Whisperer" by Donalyn Miller - Inspiring approach to creating passionate readers by giving students choice and voice in their reading lives.

- "Reading with Patrick" by Michelle Kuo - Memoir about teaching literacy that explores the transformative power of reading and the teacher-student relationship.

- "Writing Workshop" by Ralph Fletcher & JoAnn Porta Lupi - Comprehensive guide to implementing writer's workshop, helping students develop as authentic writers.

Art Education

- "Studio Thinking 2: The Real Benefits of Visual Arts Education" by Lois Hetland, Ellen Winner, Sheila Veenema & Kimberly M. Sheridan - Research-based framework identifying eight studio habits of mind (develop craft, engage & persist, envision, express, observe, reflect, stretch & explore, understand art worlds). Essential for articulating what students learn in art class.

- "Teaching Meaning in Art" by Sydney Walker - Helps teachers move beyond technique to facilitate deeper student engagement with creating and interpreting meaningful artwork.

- "The Arts and the Creation of Mind" by Elliot Eisner - Philosophical exploration of how arts education develops flexible thinking, aesthetic sensibility, and multiple forms of literacy.

- "Engaging Learners Through Artmaking" by Katherine M. Douglas and Diane B. Jaquith - Introduces "Teaching for Artistic Behavior" (TAB), a choice-based approach where students work like real artists in classroom studios.

- "Beautiful Stuff: Learning with Found Materials" by Cathy Weisman Topal and Lella Gandini - Inspired by Reggio Emilia approach, shows how to use recycled and natural materials to inspire creative exploration.

- "The Art Teacher's Survival Guide for Elementary and Middle Schools" by Helen D. Hume - Practical resource with hundreds of lesson ideas, classroom management strategies, and project instructions.

Music Education

- "A Sound Approach: Learning Through Music" by Beki Hemingway - Makes music education accessible for generalist elementary teachers with step-by-step activities and pedagogical guidance.

- "The Music Teacher's Book of Lists" by Gilbert H. Weller - Comprehensive reference with everything from composer timelines to instrument ranges to curricular standards.

- "Teaching Music Through Performance" series edited by Richard Miles - Grade-level specific volumes analyzing quality band, orchestra, and choir repertoire with teaching strategies (multiple volumes for different ensembles).

- "Musicophilia: Tales of Music and the Brain" by Oliver Sacks - Explores the neurological basis of musical experience and helps teachers understand music's profound impact on human development.

- "Music Learning Theory for Newborns and Young Children" by Edwin E. Gordon - Foundational text on audiation and sequential music learning, particularly valuable for early childhood music teachers.

- "The Relaxed Musician: Mental Preparation for Confident Performances" by Mark Duker - Addresses performance anxiety and mental skills helpful for teachers working with students preparing for recitals and auditions.

- "World Music Pedagogy" series by Patricia Shehan Campbell - Multi-volume set exploring culturally responsive approaches to teaching music from diverse global traditions.

Inclusive Education

- "Including Students with Special Needs: A Practical Guide for Classroom Teachers" by Marilyn Friend & William

Bursuck - Balanced, practical approach to inclusion with collaboration strategies.

- "UDL Now!" by Katie Novak - Universal Design for Learning principles applied practically designing instruction that's accessible from the start.

- For Early Childhood Special Education

- "DEC Recommended Practices in Early Intervention/ Early Childhood Special Education" - Gold standard practices endorsed by the Division for Early Childhood.

- "An Activity-Based Approach to Early Intervention" by Diane Bricker - Embedding learning opportunities into natural activities and routines.

Self-Care for Teachers

- "The Teacher's Guide to Self-Care" by Scott Wurdinger - Practical strategies for managing the unique stresses of special education teaching.

- "Onward" by Elena Aguilar - Resilience-building workbook helping teachers cultivate emotional resilience and avoid burnout.

Trauma-Informed Education

- "The Body Keeps the Score" by Bessel van der Kolk - Groundbreaking exploration of how trauma affects the brain and body. Essential for understanding the neuroscience behind traumatized students' behavior and learning challenges.

- "Fostering Resilient Learners" by Kristin Souers & Pete Hall - Practical guide to creating trauma-invested (not just trauma-informed) classrooms. Focuses on relationships, responsibility, and regulation with concrete classroom strategies.

- "Trauma-Sensitive Schools" by Susan Craig - Framework for building whole-school approaches to trauma. Covers universal supports, targeted interventions, and intensive individualized strategies.

- "Help for Billy" by Heather T. Forbes - Short, powerful book explaining how trauma affects student behavior and learning, with specific interventions for educators.

- "The Trauma Toolkit" by Jennifer L. Bashant - Practical strategies organized by common trauma responses. Includes reproducible tools and classroom-ready interventions.

- "Teaching the Whole Child: Instructional Practices That Support Social-Emotional Learning" by Megan Marcus and Timothy Strein - Integrates trauma-informed practices with academic instruction across content areas.

- "Helping Traumatized Children Learn" (two volumes) by Massachusetts Advocates for Children - Comprehensive framework including flexible framework, assessment tools, and practical strategies for K-12 educators.

- "Building Trauma-Sensitive Schools" by Jen Alexander - Step-by-step guide for administrators and teachers to transform school culture and practices.

Understanding Adverse Childhood Experiences (ACEs)

- "The Deepest Well" by Nadine Burke Harris - Pediatrician's exploration of how childhood adversity affects lifelong health. Explains ACEs research and biological impacts in accessible terms.

- "Childhood Disrupted" by Donna Jackson Nakazawa - Examines the long-term health consequences of childhood adversity and pathways to healing.

Brain Development and Regulation

- "The Whole-Brainchild" by Daniel Siegel and Tina Payne Bryson - Explains brain development in accessible terms with twelve practical strategies for helping children integrate experiences and develop emotional intelligence.

- "No-Drama Discipline" by Daniel Siegel and Tina Payne Bryson - Companion to above, focusing on discipline that connects rather than punishes. Teaches "connect and redirect" approach.

- "Building Resilience in Children and Teens" by Kenneth Ginsburg - Focuses on the 7 Cs of resilience (competence, confidence, connection, character, contribution, coping, control).

- "Self-Reg" by Stuart Shanker - Introduces concepts of self-regulation versus self-control. Helps educators recognize stress behaviors and support regulation rather than demanding compliance.

Social-Emotional Learning (SEL) Programs and Frameworks

- "Mindsets and Moves: Strategies That Help Readers Take Charge" by Gravity Goldberg - Practical SEL integration into reading instruction, showing how academic and social-emotional growth interconnect.

- "Social and Emotional Learning in Action" by Meena Srinivasan - Experience-based activities for building SEL competencies (self-awareness, self-management, social awareness, relationship skills, responsible decision-making).

- "Teaching with the HEART in Mind" by Lorea Martinez Perez - Practical guide to the five CASEL competencies with classroom-ready lessons and reflection tools.

- "The SEL Solution" by Jonathan C. Erwin - Integrates motivation theory with SEL, focusing on meeting students' needs for belonging, mastery, independence, and generosity.

- "Mindfulness for Teachers" by Patricia Jennings - Helps teachers develop their own mindfulness practice while learning to teach these skills to students.

- "Start Here, Start Now: A Guide to Antibias and Antiracist Work in Your School Community" by Liz Kleinrock - Connects SEL with equity and social justice. Critical for culturally responsive SEL implementation.

- "The Zones of Regulation" by Leah Kuypers - Visual, concrete framework for teaching emotional regulation using four colored zones. Includes curriculum with lessons and activities.

- "What Do You Do with a Problem?" by Kobi Yamada - Beautiful picture book (that works for all ages) about facing challenges. Great SEL teaching tool.

- "The Leader in Me" by Stephen Covey - School-wide approach based on 7 Habits, focusing on leadership and character development.

- "Yardsticks: Child and Adolescent Development Ages 4-14" by Chip Wood - Developmental characteristics by age, helping teachers have appropriate expectations and responses.

Restorative Practices

- "The Little Book of Restorative Justice" by Howard Zehr - Concise introduction to restorative justice principles and their application in schools.

- "Better Than Carrots or Sticks" by Dominique Smith, Douglas Fisher, and Nancy Frey - Practical restorative discipline strategies including affective statements, restorative questions, and community-building circles.

- "Circle Forward: Building a Restorative School Community" by Carolyn Boyes-Watson & Kay Pranis - Comprehensive guide to implementing circle practices for building community and resolving conflicts.

- "Implementing Restorative Practices in Schools" by Margaret Thorsborne and Peta Blood - Evidence-based framework for whole-school restorative approaches.

Mindfulness and Self-Regulation

- "Sitting Still Like a Frog" by Eline Snel - Simple mindfulness practices for children ages 5-12 with accompanying audio. Very teacher-friendly.

- "Mindful Teaching and Teaching Mindfulness" by Deborah Schoeberlein David - Practical guide for bringing mindfulness into classroom instruction and culture.

- "The Mindful Education Workbook" by Daniel Rechtschaffen - Lessons and activities for teaching mindfulness to students K-12.

- "Breath, Connection, Calm" by Christopher Willard - Practical strategies for bringing mindfulness and contemplative practices into schools.

Wellness for Teachers

- "Onward" by Elena Aguilar - Resilience workbook for educators. You can't pour from an empty cup. Teachers need their own SEL and trauma healing.

- "The Burnout Cure" by Chase Mielke - Practical strategies specifically for teacher wellness and sustainability.

- "Permission to Feel" by Marc Brackett - Yale researcher's guide to emotional intelligence for adults. Teachers must develop their own emotional skills to teach students.

- "Trauma Stewardship" by Laura van Dernoot Lipsky - Addresses secondary traumatic stress and compassion fatigue that affects educators working with traumatized students.

Teacher Friendly Websites

Lesson Planning & Resources

- www.teacherspayteachers.com
- www.khanacademy.org
- www.commonlit.org
- www.readwritethink.org
- www.betterlesson.com

Classroom Management

- www.classdojo.com
- www.remind.com
- classroom.google.com
- web.seesaw.me

Interactive Learning

- www.kahoot.com
- www.quizlet.com
- www.nearpod.com
- www.padlet.com
- www.flipgrid.com

Math

- www.desmos.com
- www.ixl.com
- www.mathway.com
- www.geogebra.org

- www.prodigygame.com
- www.mathigon.org
- www.illustrativemathematics.org

Science

- www.mysteryscience.com
- www.ck12.org
- www.nasa.gov/education
- www.nationalgeographic.org/education
- www.labster.com
- www.exploratorium.edu

Professional Development

- www.edutopia.org
- www.teachthought.com

Special Education

- www.understood.org
- www.pbisworld.com
- www.interventioncentral.org
- www.specialconnections.ku.edu
- www.tarheelreader.org
- www.n2y.com
- www.teacherspayteachers.com/Browse/PreK-12-Subject-Area/Special-Education -
- www.boardmakeronline.com
- www.learningally.org
- www.lessonpix.com
- www.symbolstix.com
- www.do2learn.com

- www.mayer-johnson.com
- www.ablenetinc.com
- www.council-for-exceptional-children.org
- www.wrightslaw.com
- www.autismspeaks.org/tool-kit
- www.ldaamerica.org

Physical Education

- www.pecentral.org
- www.openphysed.org
- www.peacefulplaygrounds.com
- www.sparkpe.org
- www.shapeamerica.org
- www.gophersport.com/pe
- www.thepespecialist.com
- www.choosemyplate.gov
- www.presidentschallenge.org
- www.actionforhealthykids.org
- www.cdc.gov/healthyschools/physicalactivity
- www.gomoove.org
- www.superphysicaled.com
- www.ultimatecampresource.com/camp-games
- www.playmeo.com

Music

- www.musicplayonline.com
- www.classicsforkids.com
- www.dsokids.com
- www.sfskids.org
- www.carnegiehall.org/education

- www.musictheory.net
- www.quavermusic.com
- www.smartmusic.com
- www.musicfirst.com
- www.teoria.com
- www.8notes.com
- www.noteflight.com
- www.childrensmusicworkshop.com
- www.bethsnotesplus.com
- www.musicteacherresources.com
- www.singup.org
- www.nafme.org
- www.aosa.org
- www.oake.org
- www.giml.org

Art

- www.theartofed.com
- www.artsonia.com
- www.incredibleart.org
- www.deepspacesparkle.com
- www.kinderart.com
- www.getty.edu/education
- www.metmuseum.org/learn/educators
- www.artforkidshub.com

Art History and Virtual Museums

- www.artsandculture.google.com
- www.smarthistory.org
- www.nga.gov/education

History/Social Studies

- www.loc.gov/teachers
- www.archives.gov/education
- www.primarysource.org
- www.docsteach.org
- www.ourdocuments.gov
- www.icivics.org
- www.historypin.org
- www.newsela.com
- www.facinghistory.org
- www.gilder-lehrman.org
- www.teachinghistory.org
- www.smithsonianeducation.org
- www.history.com/classroom
- www.pbs.org/education
- www.nps.gov/teachers
- www.constitutioncenter.org/learn

Differentiated Learning

- www.tarheelreader.org
- www.n2y.com
- www.teacherspayteachers.com/Browse/PreK-12-Subject-Area/Special-Education
- www.boardmakeronline.com
- www.learningally.org

Reading

- www.readingrockets.org
- www.readworks.org
- www.commonlit.org

- www.newsela.com
- www.storylineonline.net
- www.uniteforliteracy.com
- www.readtheory.org
- www.freerice.com
- www.storylineonline.net
- www.raz-kids.com
- www.epic.com
- www.starfall.com
- www.abcya.com
- www.storylineonline.net
- www.getepic.com
- www.readwritethink.org
- www.bookflix.com
- www.tumblebooks.com

English/ELA

- www.commonlit.org
- www.readwritethink.org
- www.noredink.com
- www.poetryfoundation.org
- www.literacyta.com
- www.folger.edu/teaching-shakespeare
- www.owlpurdue.edu
- www.grammaropolis.com
- www.vocabulary.com
- www.flocabulary.com
- www.achieve3000.com
- www.newseumed.org
- www.storylineonline.net

Writing

- www.writingfix.com
- www.povlib.com
- www.readwritethink.org
- www.noredink.com
- www.grammarly.com/edu
- www.hemingwayapp.com
- www.storyboardthat.com
- www.youngwritersworkshop.com
- www.writersdigest.com/be-a-better-writer
- www.nanowrimo.org/educators
- www.writingwithmrsd.com
- www.thewritesource.com
- www.dailygrammar.com

ESL/EL/ELL

- www.colorincolorado.org
- www.eslkidstuff.com
- www.eslgamesplus.com
- www.eslflow.com
- www.manythings.org
- www.usingenglish.com
- www.esl-lab.com
- www.eslgold.com
- www.mes-english.com
- www.breakingnewsenglish.com
- www.englishcentral.com
- www.duolingo.com
- www.busyteacher.org
- www.eslprintables.com

- www.englishclub.com
- www.englishforeveryone.org

Parents

- www.pbs.org/parents
- www.scholastic.com/parents
- www.understood.org
- www.naeyc.org/our-work/families
- www.zerotothree.org
- www.parenttoolkit.com
- www.readingrockets.org/family

Academic Support at Home

- www.khanacademy.org
- www.ixl.com
- www.abcmouse.com
- www.starfall.com
- www.funbrain.com
- www.coolmath.com
- www.brainpop.com
- www.kids.nationalgeographic.com

Homework Help

- www.homework.com
- www.chegg.com/tutors
- www.tutor.com
- www.wyzant.com

Parent-Teacher Communication

- www.remind.com
- www.classdojo.com
- www.bloomz.com
- www.seesaw.me

TEACHER DISCOUNTS

Here are a few helpful tips to maximize your savings. Not all discounts are available year-round, but many retailers roll out special offers during Teacher Appreciation Week in the first full week of May, so mark your calendar! Always keep your valid teacher ID handy since you'll need it to access these perks. Remember, it never hurts to ask about educator discounts, even if you don't see them advertised. You might be pleasantly surprised by what's available. Just keep in mind that offers, and eligibility can vary from state to state and location to location, so what's available in one area might not be available in another.

Technology & Electronics
- Apple - 10% off computers, iPads, and accessories
- Microsoft - 10% off Surface devices and software
- Dell - Special educator pricing on computers
- Adobe Creative Cloud - 60% off for teachers
- Lenovo - Up to 30% off for educators
- Samsung - Education discount on devices
- Verizon Wireless - Monthly discount on phone plans
- AT&T - Educator discount on wireless services

Software & Digital Tools
- Spotify Premium - 50% off for teachers
- Amazon Prime - Exclusive discounts for educators
- Canva Pro - Free for K-12 teachers
- Grammarly Premium - Educator discount available

- Evernote - Special teacher pricing
- Dropbox - Extra storage for educators

Classroom Supplies & Books
- Barnes & Noble - Teacher discount program
- Michaels - 15% off with teacher ID
- Lakeshore Learning - 15% discount
- Office Depot/OfficeMax - Teacher rewards program
- Staples - Teacher rewards with 10% back
- Scholastic - Teacher discount on book orders

Stores & Retail
- Target - 15% off twice yearly (July and back-to-school season)
- J.Crew - 15% off with valid teacher ID
- Banana Republic - 15% teacher discount
- The Container Store - 15% off with teacher ID
- Ann Taylor/LOFT - 15% teacher discount
- Clarks - Teacher discount
- Johnston & Murphy - Educator pricing
- Skechers - Teacher discount available
- New Balance - Educator discount program

Restaurants & Entertainment
- Buffalo Wild Wings - 10% teacher discount
- AMC Theatres - Discount tickets with educator ID
- Regal Cinemas - Educator discounts available
- Museums - Many offer free/discounted admission with teacher ID

About the Author

Dr. Marcia J. Millet is an award-winning educator and leader with more than 30 years of experience in K-12 and higher education. She is the president and CEO of Millet and Associates Consulting. Dr. Millet holds an Ed.D. from Tennessee State University, an M.A. from The Ohio State University, a B.S. from Bennett College, and has completed postdoctoral work at Harvard University's Women in Education Leadership Program. Her work has earned national recognition, including induction into The Ohio State University's Hall of Fame, Outstanding Alumna honors from Bennett College, and K-12 Teacher of the Year. A passionate advocate for teachers and STEM education and equity, Dr. Millet has led multimillion-dollar grant initiatives, mentored countless educators, and coordinated STEAM programs for underrepresented students.

Her research focuses on teacher preparation and retention, women in leadership, girls in STEM, and trauma-informed educational practices. Dr. Millet's mission focuses on helping educators become their "Best Selves" so they can inspire the next generation of learners.